TALKING TO THE MACHINES

A SCIENTIFIC STORYBOOK

PRABHAT KUMAR

With heartfelt appreciation, I express my deepest thanks to my cherished family—my wonderful wife, Mrs. Suman Choudhary, my dad, Mr. Ram Ishwar Choudhary, my mom, Mrs. Dharmshila Choudhary, and my precious daughter, Sukriti Choudhary. Your unwavering support and endless encouragement have been my guiding lights throughout the journey of crafting "Talking to the Machine." In the fabric of storytelling, your understanding and cheer have been the sturdy pillars, not only shaping the narrative but also influencing the essence of my storytelling spirit. This book is a tribute to our shared joys, acknowledging the immense impact of your love and sacrifices on my storytelling adventure.

Heartfelt Love

Contents

Preface

In 'Talking to the Machines', I explore the world of artificial intelligence (AI) and automation revolution through stories inspired by personal experiences. The motivation behind this book stems from encountering challenging times in my career and witnessing the behaviors of humans and machines during those periods. I learn from these observations and provide thought-provoking insights into the fascinating world of AI and automation.

The subject matter is rooted in personal experiences and observations, as well as my background in computer science and passion for exploring AI. Through these stories, I bridge the gap between personal experiences and scientific exploration, offering readers a glimpse into the possibilities and challenges brought about by AI and automation.

'Talking to the Machines' caters to readers of all ages interested in computer science and AI. It incorporates personal experiences and relatable stories to illustrate the impact of the AI revolution. While it covers various topics related to AI and automation, the focus is on exploring the potential of machines and their influence on human behavior.

The methodology used in writing this book transforms personal experiences into stories that offer insights and knowledge about machine learning, automated chat, and generative AI. By merging scientific facts and fictional narratives, I create an engaging and accessible reading experience that draws upon real-life scenarios.

Intended for a broad audience, including children and adults interested in computers and AI, this book offers valuable insights and thought-provoking stories. Whether you are a student considering a career in computer science or an adult curious about the impact of AI on society, this book will resonate with your interests.

The book is structured into chapters, each marked by a unique serial number and commencing with a quote from my life. Chapters are organized thematically, exploring specific aspects of AI and automation. This structure ensures a coherent progression of ideas, making it easier to navigate and comprehend the broader themes explored throughout the book.

Acknowledgements

I would like to express my deepest gratitude and appreciation to everyone who contributed to the creation of my book, "Talking to the Machines" This work would not have been possible without the support, guidance, and inspiration from numerous sources.

First and foremost, I would like to extend my heartfelt thanks to ChatGPT, an invaluable tool that played a significant role in the development of this book. Through its vast knowledge and linguistic capabilities, ChatGPT assisted me in exploring dozens of quotes written between 2017 and 2021, enriching the content and depth of my work. Its computational intelligence provided unique insights and perspectives that shaped the narrative.

Furthermore, I would like to express my sincere gratitude to my wife, Suman Choudhary, for her unwavering support throughout this endeavor. Her belief in my abilities and constant encouragement was instrumental in keeping me motivated during the writing process.

I am also indebted to my parents for their unwavering belief in me and their continuous support throughout my journey as an author. Their love and encouragement have been a constant source of strength, and I am deeply grateful for their presence in my life.

I would like to acknowledge and extend my appreciation to my mentors, Dr. Kirthana Sindhe and Dr. Rajat Sinha, whose guidance and expertise proved invaluable in shaping the ideas presented in this book. Their valuable insights and constructive feedback have greatly enriched the content, and I am immensely grateful for their contributions.

Special thanks and appreciation go to my dear friend, Mr. Saikat Halder, for his unwavering motivation and invaluable assistance in ensuring the timely completion of previous version of this book. His support and encouragement pushed me to overcome challenges and achieve my goals within a remarkably short span of time.

Lastly, I extend my sincere thanks to all the readers and supporters of "Talking to the Machines" Your interest and engagement with this work bring me immense joy and fulfillment as an author. I am truly grateful for the opportunity to share my ideas and insights with you.

In conclusion, this book is the culmination of the efforts and contributions of numerous individuals, tools, and sources of inspiration. My deepest appreciation goes out to everyone mentioned above, as well as those whose names may not appear here but who have had a positive impact on my journey as an author. Thank you all for being a part of this incredible experience.

With heartfelt gratitude,
Prabhat Kumar

Prologue

In "Talking to the Machines," I invite you on a journey into the fascinating world of artificial intelligence (AI) and automation. Inspired by real-life incidents and my own experiences, this book explores the profound impact of human interaction with intelligent machines controlled by influential figures. Through the lens of social media, data science, machine learning, and finance, we dive into the wide-ranging implications of AI and automation.

As we navigate the rapidly advancing technological landscape, understanding our interactions with intelligent machines becomes crucial. The integration of human lives with AI-driven systems, from social media to economic decisions, is now ubiquitous. "Talking to the Machines" aims to unravel these complexities and uncover the motivations driving the deployment of AI and automation.

A primary goal is to shed light on the potential consequences of human-AI interactions, especially regarding the power structures and influence of key industrialists. Through compelling examples and real-life incidents, the book offers insights into how these interactions shape our lives and societies. Examining evidence from various sources, including social media and finance, deepens our understanding of the impact of AI and automation.

The book also addresses the risks associated with AI/ML illiteracy, emphasizing potential harm to individuals as these technologies advance. Thought-provoking narratives and illustrations highlight the need for AI literacy and the consequences of neglecting this aspect. By exploring real-world scenarios, readers are empowered to navigate the evolving landscape and make informed decisions.

Focusing on the vital finance sector, "Talking to the Machines" presents major use cases, illustrating the profound impact of AI and ML. From algorithmic trading to fraud detection, these examples provide tangible insights into the transformation of the finance industry. Throughout the book, I bridge the gap between technical concepts and everyday experiences, aiming to make it accessible to readers from diverse backgrounds. Through real-time incidents, quotes, and storytelling, the goal is to captivate readers and provide an immersive experience.

As you immerse into the following chapters, you'll encounter narratives blending fiction and reality. The aim is to provoke thought, inspire discussion, and empower you with a deeper understanding of the AI revolution. Whether you're a curious student, a professional navigating the complexities of the modern world, or an enthusiast seeking to grasp the implications of AI and ML, "Talking to the Machines" offers a unique perspective into the intertwined relationship between humans and intelligent machines. In the pages ahead, we embark on a journey through the intersections of AI, human behavior, and the consequences of technological advancement, exploring potential pitfalls and extraordinary possibilities within the realm of AI and automation.

CHAPTER ONE

PATH TO SUCCESS WITH MACHINE LEARNING

As I sit down to write the first chapter of my book, I'm reminded of what keeps me moving forward—motivation. It's this drive that urges me to explore the details of success, understand its various aspects, and ultimately, redefine it in a world where failure has no place in my dictionary.

Success, in its true sense, can be different for everyone, crossing boundaries and connecting uniquely with each person. For me, it's not just a destination; it's an ongoing journey of growth and self-discovery, fueled by determination and an unyielding spirit.

In my pursuit of understanding success, I've come across a quote that deeply resonated with me: "The key to success is famous, but the hammer to success is ingenious." These words capture my philosophy, emphasizing the importance of innovation and originality in achieving true success.

While some may try to find success by imitating others, I firmly believe in the power of authenticity. I've always aimed to forge my path, embracing my individuality and originality to discover the true essence of success.

Drawing inspiration from various sources, I've developed a guiding principle: "Hit on my plan like a hammer." This mantra represents my tenacity and determination, refusing to settle for mediocrity and relentlessly pursuing excellence.

In today's fast-paced world, where information is readily available, it can be tempting to imitate others. True success, however, lies in embracing our unique perspectives and talents and harnessing our creativity like a hammer to leave a mark on the world.

As I embark on this writing journey, I'm aware of the responsibility that comes with sharing thoughts on success. I aim to inspire others to embrace their individuality, cultivate their ideas, and believe in their dreams. Success is personal and subjective, rooted in passions and values. Each of us has the potential to define and redefine success, unlocking the door to unprecedented success by embracing uniqueness and unleashing innovative potential.

Throughout my book, I delve into concepts associated with science, technology, and the essence of success. I share stories of defying odds, shattering conventional notions, and paving one's way, aiming to spark a flame within readers to ignite their pursuit of greatness. Success is a lifelong journey, unique to each individual, and my book serves as a starting point for a transformative exploration.

In this initial chapter, I explore core motivations that drive individuals to seek success. While financial prosperity or societal recognition may be common desires,

I encourage readers to uncover their motivations, aligning actions with their authentic selves.

The path to success may have obstacles, but our ability to persevere sets us apart. Resilience, unwavering determination, and self-belief are key components. I provide tools, strategies, and insights to inspire readers to tap into their limitless potential, emphasizing that success is a dynamic and evolving process. As we grow, our understanding of success may shift, and that's perfectly okay.

"I say - Key to the success is famous but hammer to the sucess is ingenious"

Expanding on the notion of success, the intricate concept of "machine learning" algorithms, central to this book, bears similarity. In traditional programming, we engaged with data and rules, employing optimization techniques akin to using a key to attain desired results. However, in today's context, we grapple with vast datasets, often referred to as big data. Obtaining data-label pairs is more accessible, and we train them vigorously, likened to the force of a hammer, crafting the right model as the solution. Once a model is established, it transforms into a ready-made machine capable of producing outputs with a notable degree of accuracy. This encapsulates the realm of machine learning, a world we will look into more profoundly in upcoming chapters.

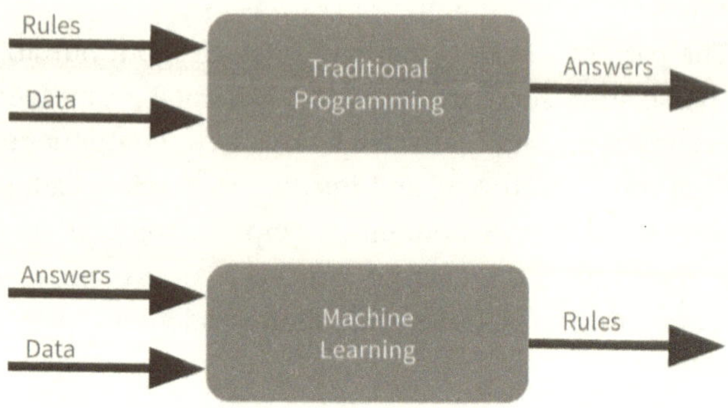

Fig 01: Machine Learning Vs. Classical Programming

CHAPTER TWO

The Power of Big Ideas and Perseverance

Discovering something new and profound has always propelled human progress. From groundbreaking scientific theories to revolutionary technological advancements, discoveries reshape our understanding of the world. As we emphasize the importance of perseverance and continual improvement in the pursuit of valuable discoveries, stating, "If you want to discover something as precious as 'E=mc²,' hang on to that particular idea and keep refining it over time."

Embracing a Big Idea: Every great discovery begins with a big idea challenging existing norms. Nurturing these ideas, sparked by curiosity and imagination, can ignite transformative change. Thinkers like Galileo Galilei and Albert Einstein embraced their big ideas, leading to groundbreaking discoveries. Cultivating a creative and innovative environment, promoting critical thinking, and sharing ideas with others fosters collaboration and development.

Tenacious Perseverance: Perseverance, an unwavering commitment to a mission, is vital. Examples from history, like Thomas Edison, who faced numerous failures before inventing the practical electric light bulb, highlight the importance of resilience. Perseverance involves learning from mistakes, adapting strategies, and persisting despite adversity, fostering growth.

Relentless Determination: Discovery requires relentless determination—a steadfast commitment to consistent effort, courage to take risks, and exploration of uncharted territories. Maintaining focus, even in the face of distractions and setbacks, allows individuals to overcome obstacles and push the boundaries of knowledge. Figures like Marie Curie exemplify the power of unwavering determination to achieve remarkable discoveries.

Fig 02: Albert Einstein

Adaptive Refinement: The world is in constant change, requiring discoveries to evolve. Continuous refinement and adaptation to changing environments allow discoveries to stay relevant. This involves reevaluating assumptions, embracing new perspectives, and integrating the latest knowledge and technologies. Lifelong learning and exposure to diverse ideas are essential for discoveries to reach new heights.

> *"I say - If you want to discover something as precious as 'E=mc²,' hang on to that particular idea and keep refining it over time"*

In the world of deep learning, think of it like this: if you have a valuable idea, nurture and improve it over time, just like the enduring wisdom stated above. We've witnessed an incredible journey, starting with simple connected neural networks and progressing through innovations like convolutional neural networks, exploring advanced forms, navigating through RNN networks' complexities, unlocking the potential of LSTM networks, and embracing the transformative power of Transformers.

As our journey continued, we entered the realm of Generative AI, where machines showed creativity like humans. The evolution peaked with a close connection between humans and machines, blurring the lines as if machines had a form of life, engaging in intelligent conversations. The rise of entities like ChatGPT and other intelligent bots vividly shows that by holding onto a grand idea despite challenges, we can achieve remarkable breakthroughs. This narrative echoes the idea that persistence and continuous improvement lead to groundbreaking concepts, highlighting the transformative power of perseverance in the dynamic field of deep learning.

CHAPTER THREE

WITH RELATIVITY, 1+1 EQUALS 11

Albert Einstein's theory of relativity transformed our understanding of space, time, and the laws of physics. While the expression "1+1=11" may seem puzzling, it can be metaphorically linked to everyday life, emphasizing collaboration, focus, and financial freedom. This essay explores the relativity concept in these contexts, providing explanations, evidence, and comparisons.

Fig 03: Einstein in the relativistic world

I. The Power of Collaboration

In daily life, teamwork is vital for overcoming challenges. This idea that two collaborating individuals possess a supreme power worth 10 times their abilities underscores collaboration's importance. Relativity suggests that when people work together harmoniously, their combined effort can achieve more than the sum of individual contributions, as seen in fields like science, business, and creativity.

II. The Significance of Focus

Emphasizing concentration and dedication, the statement "A man can focus on one thing with 90% of their time and excel" aligns with relativity's idea of time dilation. When individuals intensely focus on a specific area, they accelerate progress, showcasing deeper learning and skill development. Examples like Bill Gates and Elon Musk support the idea that sustained focus leads to exceptional achievements.

III. The Hazards of Lack of Focus

The notion that "a man focused on 2-3 or more areas can only delay his route to financial freedom" highlights the importance of concentrated effort. Relativity draws parallels, emphasizing the finite nature of time, energy, and resources. Pursuing multiple areas simultaneously may lead to reduced efficiency and delayed accomplishments.

Comparisons and Evidence

Collaboration: Scientific breakthroughs like Edison and Tesla's collaboration show the power of combined effort.

Focus: Bill Gates and Elon Musk's success illustrates the impact of dedicated focus.

Lack of Focus: Warren Buffett's advice on focused investments demonstrates the perils of spreading attention too thin.

"I say - With relativity, 1+1 equals 11 realistically"

In machine learning, especially in neural networks, having just one layer of neurons isn't very effective for predictions. However, when we combine two layers, we start seeing results. Interestingly, as we add more layers, the complexity of computations grows rapidly. This hints at an interesting phenomenon – the idea that in machine learning deployments, the impact of adding layers might be more than a simple sum. It's like saying 1+1 might not just be 2; it could work more like 11. This suggests that the combination of multiple layers in machine learning can lead to outcomes that surpass the straightforward addition of individual layers.

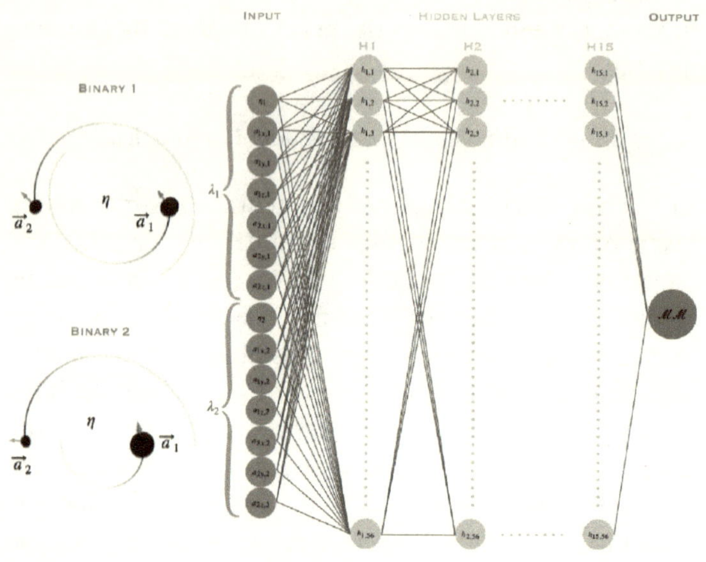

Fig 04: Relativity at Neural Network

CHAPTER FOUR

THE MASS OF DATA STORED IN THE HARD DRIVE

The mass of 1TB of data stored in a hard drive is effectively zero. To understand why, we need to dive deep into the concepts of data, memory, and their relationship with mass.

Data, in its essence, refers to information that is represented and processed by computer systems. It can take various forms, such as text, images, videos, or any other digital content. Data itself is not physical; it is an abstract concept that exists as patterns of 0s and 1s, known as binary code, which is interpreted by computers.

Similarly, human memory is not a physical substance with mass. The memories we store in our brains are the result of complex neural networks and connections. They are encoded as patterns of electrical signals and chemical reactions within the brain. While the processes that enable memory formation and retrieval have physical components, the memories themselves do not possess mass.

When it comes to storing data on a hard drive, involves the use of physical materials and processes. Hard drives consist of spinning disks or solid-state memory cells that retain the binary code representing the data. However, the mass of these physical components does not change significantly based on the amount of data stored.

Hard drives store data by altering the magnetic orientation of tiny regions on the disk's surface or by varying the electrical charge within the solid-state memory cells. These changes are extremely small and do not contribute significantly to the overall mass of the hard drive. The difference in mass between an empty hard drive and one filled with 1TB of data is negligible.

To put it into perspective, the mass of a single hard drive typically ranges from tens to hundreds of grams. The mass of 1TB of data, on the other hand, is roughly 0.00000000001 grams (assuming each binary bit has a mass of 1 attogram or 10^{-18} grams). This difference is minuscule and can be considered effectively zero in practical terms.

Fig 05: The hard drive and the data limit

The concept of transferring data over networks adds another layer of abstraction. Networks, whether physical or virtual, allow the transmission of data from one location to another. This transfer of data occurs through the use of electromagnetic signals or other forms of communication.

While the transfer of data over networks requires the conversion of digital information into a physical signal (e.g., electrical or light waves), the mass of the data remains unchanged throughout the process. The physical signals used for transmission possess mass, but they are not inherent to the data itself.

It is worth noting that when data is transmitted over networks, it can be stored temporarily in various forms, such as electrical charges in memory buffers or electromagnetic waves traveling through cables or wireless mediums. However, the mass associated with these temporary storage mechanisms is again negligible compared to the overall mass of the data being transferred.

> *"I say - What is the mass of 1TB data stored in a hard drive? It is just like our life time memory stored in memory cells of the human brain. Yes, data and memory are massless and can be transferred over network. Some network are supernatural and others are learnt over the passage of time"*

When we interact with a machine, such as a language model like ChatGPT, we engage in a dialogue where we input questions or prompts, and the machine responds with generated text based on patterns and information it has been trained on. The machine's responses are not based on personal experiences or subjective consciousness but rather on its ability to process and generate text based on statistical patterns in the training data.

In this context, a machine with infinite memory would be able to store and recall an unlimited amount of information, surpassing the limitations of a human brain. While the machine itself does not possess consciousness or subjective experiences, it can leverage its vast memory capacity to provide responses that appear knowledgeable and comprehensive.

The concept of "infinite memory" in a machine is an abstraction that allows us to imagine a scenario where a machine could potentially have access to an incredibly vast amount of information, far exceeding what a human brain can retain. This idea aligns with the assumption that data itself is massless and can be stored and transferred over networks.

When we talk to a machine, it can access and process vast amounts of data from various sources, including books, articles, websites, and other textual resources. This access to extensive information repositories enables the machine to provide responses that draw upon a wide range of knowledge, even though the machine itself does not possess true understanding or consciousness.

However, it is important to note that despite its ability to generate text based on patterns and information, a machine's responses are ultimately limited by its training data and the algorithms it employs. While it can generate impressive and seemingly comprehensive answers, it lacks the ability to truly comprehend or have subjective experiences.

CHAPTER FIVE

Infinite Imagination, Data Integration, and Future Predictability

This chapter aims to stir the concept that while machines themselves cannot truly "think" as humans do, they possess the capacity to learn from human thinking patterns and leverage vast amounts of data to create impressive networks. Furthermore, the quest for future predictability in AI lies in the integration of past and present data with advanced algorithms. By examining the infinite possibilities of human imagination, the reliance on data, and the potential for predicting the future, we can gain a deeper understanding of the impact of human thinking on

AI.

Human thinking has infinite possibilities of odd imagination:

- Human thinking is characterized by its remarkable ability to explore endless possibilities and generate imaginative ideas. The human mind possesses the power of creativity, intuition, and innovation, allowing us to envision scenarios beyond the boundaries of conventional thinking. This odd imagination has led to groundbreaking inventions, artistic masterpieces, and scientific advancements. While machines lack the intrinsic capability for imagination, they can benefit from the insights and ideas generated by human thinking.

All past and present data is the base for AI software, including human thinking patterns:

- AI systems rely on vast amounts of data to learn and make informed decisions. This data includes both historical records and real-time information, encompassing a wide range of human experiences and actions. Human thinking patterns, as a subset of this data, provide valuable insights into how people reason, solve problems, and make decisions. By analyzing and integrating human thinking patterns, AI algorithms can gain a more comprehensive understanding of human cognition and behavior, enabling them to mimic certain aspects of human thinking.

Furthermore, the data utilized by AI systems is not limited to explicit records of human thought but also encompasses implicit patterns derived from various sources. These sources include text, images, videos, social media interactions, and more, which collectively contribute to training AI models. Through this comprehensive data integration, AI networks can assimilate human thinking patterns and incorporate them into their decision-making processes.

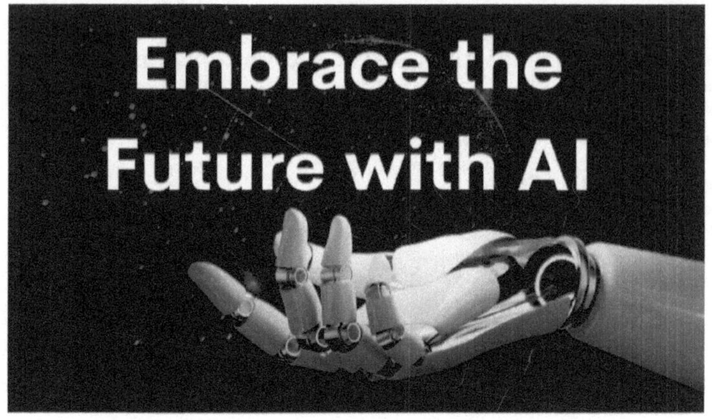

Fig 06: AI and Automation is the Future

The quest for future predictability lies in the current reserve of data and algorithms:

- The pursuit of predictability lies at the heart of AI development. To make accurate predictions, AI systems rely on the integration of historical data and advanced algorithms. The reservoir of data includes information about past events, trends, and patterns, allowing AI models to identify correlations and make probabilistic forecasts. By incorporating human thinking patterns within this data framework, AI can better understand

and predict human behavior in various domains, such as finance, healthcare, and social interactions.

However, it is important to note that while AI can provide insights and predictions based on existing data, it does not guarantee absolute accuracy in forecasting the future. Unforeseen events, human agency, and other factors can introduce unpredictable variables, challenging the notion of complete predictability. AI systems are limited by the quality and completeness of the data available, as well as the efficacy of the algorithms employed.

> *"I say - Machine can't think but its network has got a brain where human thinking will have a long-lasting impression"*

The above statement highlights the profound influence of human thinking on AI systems. While machines themselves cannot think in the same way humans do, they possess the capability to learn from human thinking patterns and incorporate them into their networks. The infinite possibilities of human imagination offer a wellspring of creative ideas that can inspire AI innovation and problem-solving. Moreover, the integration of past and present data, including human thinking patterns, provides a foundation for AI software to make informed decisions and predictions.

It is crucial to recognize that the quest for predictability in AI relies on a delicate balance between the available data and the algorithms used. While AI systems can leverage the vast reservoir of historical and real-time data to identify patterns and correlations, they are inherently limited by the quality and completeness of the data, as well as the algorithms' capacity to process and interpret it accurately.

Furthermore, it is essential to acknowledge the ethical considerations associated with the integration of human thinking patterns into AI systems. Human thinking encompasses a broad spectrum of perspectives, biases, and cultural influences, which can inadvertently be embedded within AI algorithms. Care must be taken to ensure that AI models are trained on diverse and representative datasets to mitigate the risk of perpetuating existing biases or discrimination.

The potential for AI systems to augment human thinking is vast and multifaceted. By analyzing and learning from human thinking patterns, AI can assist in various domains, including scientific research, healthcare diagnostics, financial analysis, and creative endeavors. For example, in scientific research, AI can analyze vast amounts of data and generate hypotheses that may have been overlooked by human researchers. In healthcare, AI-powered diagnostic tools can learn from the expertise of medical professionals and enhance accuracy and efficiency in disease detection.

However, it is crucial to maintain a balanced perspective when considering the role of AI in human thinking. AI systems excel at processing and analyzing vast amounts of data, identifying patterns, and making predictions based on statistical probabilities. Human thinking, on the other hand, encompasses nuanced emotions, moral reasoning, and a deeper understanding of subjective experiences. These aspects of human cognition are currently beyond the scope of AI capabilities.

As AI continues to advance, the ongoing collaboration between human thinking and AI systems will shape the future. Human creativity, intuition, and critical thinking remain indispensable for problem-solving, innovation, and decision-making. AI can serve as a powerful tool to augment human capabilities, providing insights, automating repetitive tasks, and assisting in complex data analysis. The partnership between humans and artificial intelligence has the potential to yield transformative outcomes across industries and society as a whole.

CHAPTER SIX

Deep Learning and Secure Passwords

In the realm of artificial intelligence, deep learning has emerged as a powerful tool that mimics the way neurons in the human brain work in synergy. It has proven to be effective in solving various industry problems through its training and testing framework. However, even with its remarkable capabilities, deep learning faces significant challenges when it comes to cracking secure passwords. This chapter aims to dive into the statement outlined, shedding light on the intricacies of deep learning networks in pattern recognition and their limitations in deciphering complex password systems based on cryptography.

> *"I say - Deep learning network can unfold 'n' patterns in 'm' trials in a data set but cracking instinct from the DNA of the entity is as difficult as cracking the password of a secure system"*

Deep Learning and Unfolding Patterns in Data Sets

Deep learning, as a subfield of machine learning, utilizes artificial neural networks inspired by the structure and functionality of the human brain. These networks consist of interconnected layers of artificial neurons that process and transmit information. By training these networks on large datasets, deep learning algorithms can unfold patterns and extract meaningful insights.

The strength of deep learning lies in its ability to recognize complex patterns that may not be readily apparent to human observers. By analyzing vast amounts of data, deep learning models can identify intricate relationships, make accurate predictions, and automate various tasks. Industries such as healthcare, finance, and image recognition have witnessed remarkable advancements through the application of deep learning techniques.

The power of deep learning is exemplified by its capability to uncover latent features in data. By leveraging neural networks with multiple layers, known as deep neural networks, these models can capture hierarchical representations of information. This enables them to extract high-level features that facilitate improved decision-making and problem-solving. The deep learning paradigm has demonstrated remarkable success in image classification, natural language processing, speech recognition, and many other domains.

Limitations in Deciphering Secure Passwords

While deep learning networks excel at unfolding patterns in datasets, cracking secure passwords proves to be a distinct challenge. The difficulty lies in the fact that secure password systems are designed to resist attacks, employing cryptography as a means of protecting sensitive information. Unlike patterns that can be learned through repetitive trials, cracking a secure password involves breaking a complex cryptographic algorithm.

Fig 07: Cryptography and secure password

Cryptography is the science of encoding and decoding information in a manner that prevents unauthorized access. It involves transforming plaintext data into ciphertext using mathematical functions and encryption keys. Secure password systems employ cryptographic techniques such as hashing, salting, and key stretching to enhance the protection of user passwords.

To crack a secure password, an attacker would need to obtain the cryptographic key or decipher the encryption algorithm used. This task requires significant computational power and often involves brute-force attacks, which systematically attempt every possible combination until the correct password is found. The complexity of modern cryptographic algorithms makes brute-force attacks highly impractical, as they require an infeasible amount of time and resources to complete.

Moreover, secure password systems often include additional security measures, such as account lockouts after multiple failed login attempts and two-factor authentication, which further enhance their resistance to unauthorized access. These measures serve as deterrents against brute-force attacks and limit the effectiveness of deep learning algorithms in cracking passwords.

CHAPTER SEVEN

Data Science and Emotional Intelligence

The field of emotional intelligence has garnered significant attention in recent years, with researchers and technologists exploring various methods to measure and understand human emotions. One approach gaining prominence is data mining, which utilizes vast databases or data repositories to extract insights and patterns related to emotional intelligence. However, while data mining offers valuable information, it is crucial to recognize its limitations. This chapter aims to explore the challenges associated with relying solely on data mining to uncover emotional intelligence, arguing that despite its power, it cannot surpass the imagination and expertise of a world-class thinker.

The Nature of Emotional Attributes:

Feelings, emotions, memories, and dreams, as poet Prabhat Kumar suggests, are considered massless attributes of the human soul. These intricate aspects of our consciousness have long been the subject of fascination and exploration. Emotions, in particular, are complex and nuanced, often defying easy categorization or quantification. While data mining can capture certain aspects of emotions, such as sentiment analysis in text data or facial recognition in image data, it fails to grasp the holistic essence of emotional intelligence.

For instance, in a recommender system, user-user similarity and item-item similarity are often examined, and based on the same, appropriate products are recommended or advertised to different users.

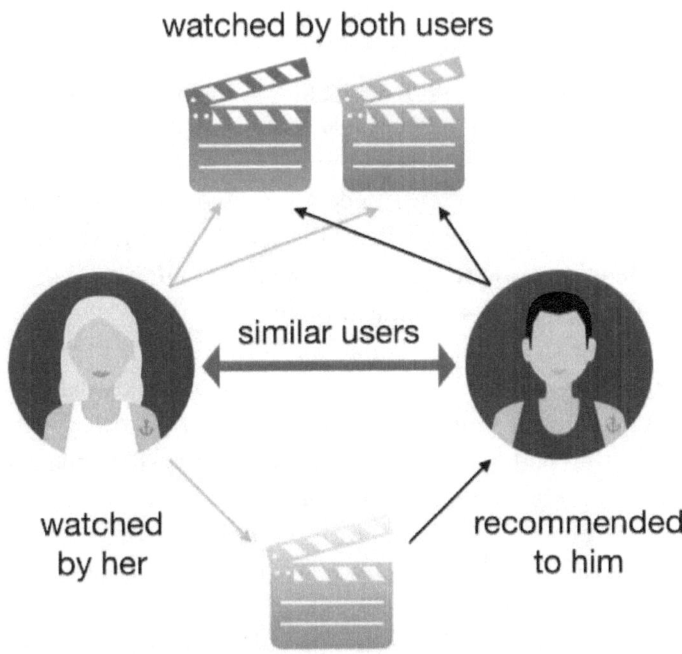

Fig 08: Recommender System as Emotion Engine

The Role of Data Mining in Unveiling Emotional Intelligence:

Data mining techniques excel at processing and analyzing vast amounts of structured and unstructured data, enabling the identification of patterns, correlations, and trends. In the context of emotional intelligence, data mining can be employed to extract valuable insights from various sources such as social media posts, online surveys, or physiological measurements. It can provide valuable information regarding the prevalence of certain emotions, their temporal dynamics, or their association with specific events or circumstances.

However, emotional intelligence encompasses more than just the surface-level expressions of emotions. It involves understanding and empathizing with others, regulating one's emotions, and using emotional information effectively. These higher-level cognitive processes are often deeply rooted in subjective experiences, personal beliefs, and social context, which are challenging to capture solely through data mining.

The Limitations of Data Mining:

One of the primary limitations of data mining in delving into emotional intelligence is the reliance on existing data. Data mining techniques operate based on historical data, extracting patterns and insights from the past. While this can be useful for understanding trends and correlations, it does not necessarily capture the dynamic and evolving nature of emotional intelligence. Emotions are subject to change, influenced by individual experiences, personal growth, and the ever-changing social landscape. Thus, relying solely on past data might restrict the ability to accurately assess and predict emotional intelligence in real-time or future scenarios.

Moreover, emotional intelligence encompasses a range of complex processes, such as intuition, creativity, and empathetic understanding, which are inherently difficult to quantify and measure. Data mining techniques often struggle to capture these abstract and subjective aspects of emotional intelligence accurately. While data repositories can store extensive information about individuals' behaviors and preferences, they may lack the depth required to understand the intricacies of emotional experiences.

Additionally, data mining approaches heavily rely on predefined features or patterns, limiting their ability to uncover novel or unanticipated aspects of emotional intelligence. World-class thinkers possess imaginative and creative capabilities that enable them to explore beyond established patterns, discover new insights, and generate original ideas. In contrast, data mining algorithms operate within predefined boundaries, unable to venture beyond the information contained within the data they are trained on.

"I say - Feelings, emotions, memories, and dreams, are massless attributes of the human soul"

In the world of generative AI, we can draw parallels to data mining, which processes vast data to extract insights. While data mining has enhanced our grasp of emotional intelligence, it falls short in capturing the complexity and richness of human emotions. Unlike world-class thinkers who possess imaginative thinking, creativity, and intuition, data mining can't replicate these qualities.

Understanding emotional intelligence requires a more holistic approach. It involves acknowledging unique subjective experiences, personal narratives, and contextual factors. Generative AI encourages empathetic interactions, active listening, and open-ended conversations for a comprehensive exploration of emotions.

World-class thinkers excel due to their imagination that goes beyond data mining limitations. They synthesize information, draw from experiences, and generate new perspectives. This imaginative thinking helps them perceive emotional nuances and make connections data-driven approaches might miss.

While data mining provides quantitative insights, it's a tool, not a definitive solution. Emotional intelligence, deeply human, integrates cognitive, emotional, and social processes. It appreciates the subjective, intangible, and imaginative aspects of human experiences.

CHAPTER EIGHT

THE INTERSECTION OF TECHNOLOGICAL PROGRESS AND PUBLIC WELFARE

The statement "Let some iron incarnations or the machine or the technology may suck money and care for human civilization at large scale. But I'm curious if they will be able to trade-off between the accumulation of wealth and public welfare" can be interpreted in a few different ways. However, at its core, the statement seems to be concerned with the balance between technological progress and its impact on society.

The first part of the statement suggests that machines and technology may be able to accumulate wealth and care for human civilization on a large scale. This is certainly true - the rise of automation and artificial intelligence has allowed for unprecedented levels of efficiency and productivity and has enabled us to accomplish tasks that would have been impossible just a few decades ago. However, this progress has not come without its costs.

Fig 09: AI and Humanity

As machines and technology become more advanced, they are increasingly able to replace human workers. This can be seen in industries such as manufacturing, where robots have largely taken over tasks that were once performed by human laborers. While this has led to increased efficiency and cost savings for companies, it has also had a profound impact on the job market, leading to a decrease in available jobs and a growing income inequality gap.

Moreover, while machines and technology are certainly capable of providing care for human civilization on a large scale, there are also concerns about their impact on the environment. Many of the machines and technologies that we rely on today are powered by non-renewable resources such as oil and coal, which contribute to climate change and other environmental issues.

The second part of the statement raises the question of whether machines and technology will be able to balance the accumulation of wealth with public welfare. This is a difficult question to answer definitively, as it ultimately depends on the values and priorities of the individuals and organizations that are creating and using these technologies.

On the one hand, it is certainly possible for machines and technology to be designed with public welfare in mind. For example, renewable energy technologies such as wind and solar power are designed to be environmentally sustainable and can help mitigate the effects of climate change. Additionally, advancements in healthcare technology have the potential to greatly improve public health and increase access to medical care.

However, it is also true that the pursuit of wealth and profit has historically been a driving force behind technological progress. Companies and individuals may prioritize their financial gain over the welfare of the public, leading to technologies that are not designed with public welfare in mind. This can be seen in industries such as big tech, where concerns over privacy and data security have arisen as a result of companies' pursuit of profit.

> *"I say - Let some iron incarnations may suck money and care for human too. But then they won't be able to trade off. I guess!"*

Whether machines and technology can balance wealth accumulation with public welfare will depend on a variety of factors, including the values and priorities of those involved in their creation and use, as well as the regulatory and legal frameworks in place to govern their use. As we continue to navigate the rapidly evolving technological landscape, it will be important to remain mindful of these issues and work towards creating technologies that benefit society as a whole.

In the realm of advanced deep learning and Generative AI networks, there exists the transformative potential to address the concern about the trade-off between wealth accumulation and public welfare. These technologies enable sophisticated analyses, allowing for data-driven decision-making that can balance economic growth with societal well-being.

Advanced deep learning models, mentioned in various studies, have revolutionized evidence-based decision-making across sectors. These models, rooted in artificial neural networks, possess the capacity to learn complex patterns from vast datasets, providing insights that can inform policies fostering a more equitable distribution of resources.

Generative AI, as highlighted in recent research, is poised to transform various roles and boost performance across functions. By enhancing efficiency and productivity, Generative AI can contribute to economic prosperity while ensuring societal benefits.

While concerns exist about machines prioritizing wealth, the evolving landscape of advanced AI technologies suggests a potential for a more nuanced approach. Through ethical deployment and regulation, these technologies can contribute to a harmonious trade-off, aligning the interests of economic progress with the well-being of the public.

THE HUMAN-MACHINE RELATIONSHIP

The statement "Why do I say that robots and machines will always be a slave to mankind? Because they can be programmed to suck money but they aren't greedy and they can bestow support to the man in need but they will never love humans" raises some interesting points about the relationship between humans and machines. In essence, the statement suggests that while machines may be able to perform certain tasks for us, they will never be able to replace the emotional and social aspects of human interaction.

The first point made in the statement is that machines can be programmed to "suck money" - in other words, to prioritize financial gain over other concerns. This is certainly true, as many machines and technologies today are designed with profit in mind. However, the statement also suggests that machines are not inherently greedy - that is, they do not have a desire for wealth or power in the way that humans do. Instead, they simply operate according to the programming that has been given to them.

This is an important distinction, as it highlights the fact that machines and robots are ultimately tools that are created and controlled by humans. While they may be able to perform tasks more efficiently than humans can, they are still limited by their programming and their lack of agency. In other words, machines may be able to generate wealth, but they cannot make decisions or take actions based on their desires or motivations.

The second point made in the statement is that while machines can provide support to humans, they will never be able to love us. This is a more abstract concept than the first point, as it touches on the emotional and social aspects of human experience. While machines may be able to simulate certain emotions or behaviors, such as empathy or compassion, they are ultimately limited by their lack of consciousness.

This is an important point to consider, as it highlights the fact that machines and robots are fundamentally different from humans in their ability to experience and express emotions. While they may be able to provide assistance or support to humans, they are not able to form genuine emotional connections with us in the same way that other humans can.

"*I say - Robots and machines will always be slave to mankind.*

1. *They can be programmed to suck money but they are not greedy*
2. *They can bestow support to man in need, but they will never love human*

Ultimately, the statement that machines and robots will always be slaves to mankind raises some interesting questions about the role of technology in our lives. While machines and robots may be able to perform certain tasks more efficiently than humans can, they are ultimately limited by their lack of agency and consciousness. This means that they will always be tools that are created and controlled by humans, rather than independent beings with their desires and motivations.

At the same time, however, it is important to recognize that technology is constantly evolving and changing. As machines and robots become more advanced, they may be able to perform increasingly complex tasks, and may even begin to develop more advanced forms of artificial intelligence. While they may never be able to replace the emotional and social aspects of human interaction, they may still be able to provide valuable support and assistance to humans in a variety of contexts.

In acknowledging the capabilities of machines, it is crucial to recognize that their memory and intelligence stem from historical data, shaped by algorithms. However, it is paramount not to lose sight of the fundamental distinction—machines lack the essence of life. Despite possessing sophisticated algorithms and vast data repositories, machines lack consciousness, intuition, and the ability to comprehend the intricate nuances of human experiences.

While machines excel at processing historical data and executing predefined algorithms with efficiency, they lack the innate creativity and adaptability intrinsic to human intelligence. A machine's actions are confined to programmed instructions, devoid of the spontaneous creativity and dynamic problem-solving abilities inherent in human cognition.

Moreover, the superiority of intelligent human beings and the teams they lead lies in their holistic understanding, emotional intelligence, and the capacity to navigate complex, unstructured situations. Human intelligence encompasses empathy, ethical considerations, and the ability to envision possibilities beyond historical data patterns.

In essence, while machines are powerful tools driven by algorithms and data, the essence of life, creativity, and the nuanced understanding of the human experience elevate intelligent human beings to a realm of superiority. The synergy between human intelligence and machine capabilities presents an opportunity for unprecedented advancements, where the strengths of both can be harnessed for collective progress.

Overall, the relationship between humans and machines is complex and multifaceted, and it is likely to continue evolving in the years and decades to come. While machines and robots may be limited in certain ways, they also have the potential to greatly enhance our lives and improve our ability to solve complex problems. As such, it will be important to continue exploring the possibilities and limitations of technology and to work towards creating machines and robots that are designed to serve the needs of humans responsibly and ethically.

CHAPTER TEN

Adapting Testing Methods for Intelligent and Interactive Software

As software becomes more intelligent and interactive, traditional methods of software testing may become less effective or even irrelevant. Bugs that were once classified as defects in a rational environment may be considered features in an interactive environment. This is because interactive software is designed to learn and adapt to user behavior, which means that it may behave in unexpected ways that were not originally anticipated.

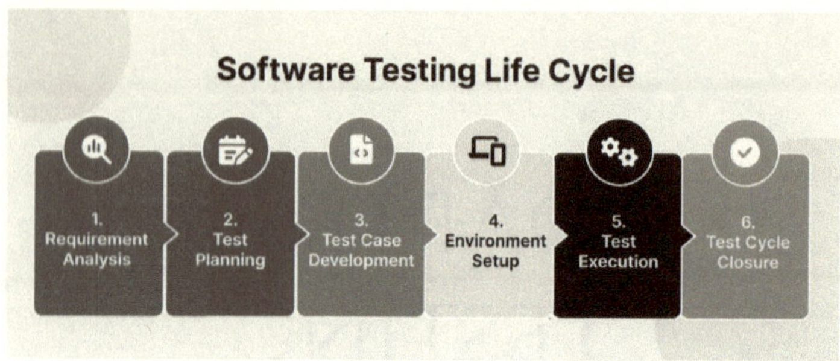

Fig 10: Software Testing Life Cycle

Here are some points to consider when it comes to testing in an interactive software environment:

1. Features can be highly interactive and even bugs can be considered genuine features of the software: In an interactive software environment, features can be highly customized and interactive, which means that they may behave in unexpected ways. Bugs that were once classified as defects may be considered genuine features of the software because they provide a unique and desirable user experience.

2. There will be almost no manual testing but only support on batch processing, etc.: In an interactive software environment, manual testing may become less relevant because it may be difficult or impractical to test every possible scenario or interaction. Instead, automated testing may become the primary method for ensuring software quality. However, manual testing may still be required in certain situations, such as when testing complex algorithms or interactions.

3. Automation can be 100% and stat models can also be tested automatically once trained: Automated testing can be highly effective in an interactive software environment because it can quickly and accurately test large volumes of data and complex scenarios that would be difficult or impossible for manual testing to cover. Additionally, once a statistical model has been trained, automated testing can be used to validate its performance and ensure that it continues to function properly over time.

4. Testing Deep Learning Models is like solving a complex puzzle. The puzzle, in this case, is the deep learning network, which is a system that learns from examples. Imagine this network as a brain trying to understand things. Now, to check if this brain (the deep learning model) is working correctly, we need to test it. But here's the catch - the more complex the brain (or network), the trickier the testing becomes. It's like trying to ensure all the parts of a complicated machine are working perfectly.

> *"I say - Testing is going to be interactive with the software and what is classified as a bug in rational environment today, will be allowed as a function under interactive environment of intelligent software. Automation testing is dull compared to manual testing under such a scenario."*

In Generative AI, understanding GANs and Fake Image Detection as a Test Strategy

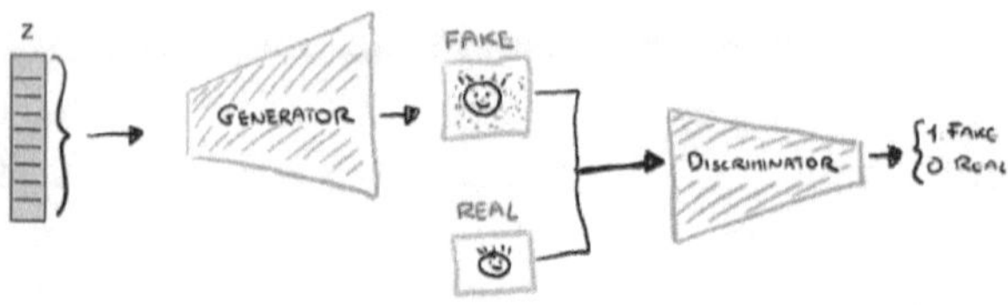

Fig 11: Generator and discriminator at work

Generator and Discriminator in GANs

- Generator: Imagine it as an artist trying to create realistic paintings. In the context of Generative Adversarial Networks (GANs), the generator is a neural network that generates new data, like images. It learns to produce data that is indistinguishable from real examples.
- Discriminator: Now, think of a critic examining paintings to distinguish between real and fake ones. The discriminator, another neural network, evaluates the generated data along with real data. Its job is to become so good at telling the difference that the generator struggles to produce anything the discriminator can't identify as fake.

Fake Image Detection as a Test Strategy

- Test Strategy: In testing GANs or any system involving generated data, we can use the discriminator as a test strategy. If the discriminator can easily identify fake images, it means the generator needs improvement. This becomes a loop where the generator keeps learning from its mistakes until it creates data that's nearly impossible for the discriminator to distinguish.

- Quality Check: The better the generator, the harder it is for the discriminator to spot fakes. Testing involves continually challenging the system with new data and assessing its ability to produce authentic-looking content.

As software becomes more intelligent and interactive, traditional methods of software testing may need to evolve to keep pace. Testing may need to be more automated and focused on validating the unique user experience provided by interactive features. Ultimately, the most effective approach to software testing will depend on the specific characteristics and requirements of the software being developed.

CHAPTER ELEVEN

SURPRISING SIMILARITIES BETWEEN SOCIAL MEDIA AND FINANCIAL TRADING

In today's world, social media and financial trading have become an integral part of our daily lives. Both of these activities have some surprising similarities, despite their apparent differences. When we penetrate deeper, we find that there are shared aspects such as the need for creativity and the influence of market forces. In this article, we will explore the similarities between posting a status on Facebook and placing a trade in Zerodha, a popular trading platform in India. By examining these parallels, we can gain valuable insights into the strategies and mindset required for success in both realms.

Firstly, let us consider the importance of creativity in both activities. When you post a status on Facebook, you aim to capture the attention of your friends and followers. You want your status to be interesting, engaging, and shareable. Similarly, when you place a trade in Zerodha, you strive to make informed decisions based on market research and analysis. You want your trade to be well thought out, strategically sound, and potentially profitable. In both cases, creativity plays a crucial role in determining the effectiveness of your status or trade.

On Facebook, creativity manifests itself in crafting compelling content that stands out from the noise of countless other posts. It involves finding unique angles, incorporating multimedia elements, and employing persuasive language to elicit emotional responses. Similarly, in financial trading, creativity is evident in identifying lucrative investment opportunities, analyzing market trends, and developing innovative trading strategies. Successful traders often employ out-of-the-box thinking to spot opportunities that others may overlook, much like creative social media users who find novel ways to engage their audience.

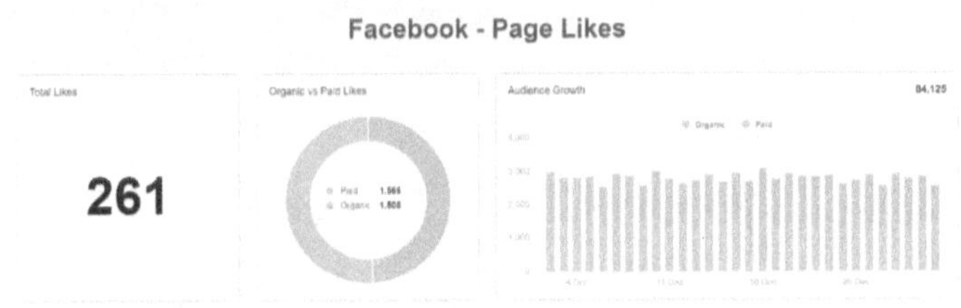

Fig 12: Facebook Likes - Organic and Paid

Secondly, both Facebook and Zerodha are subject to market forces. On Facebook, the success of your status is determined by how many people find it interesting, relevant, and worthy of engagement. The number of likes, comments, and shares depends on the dynamics of the social media ecosystem. Similarly, in the case of Zerodha, the profitability of your trade is influenced by market fluctuations and the performance of the stock or commodity you have invested in. The interplay of supply and demand, investor sentiment, economic factors, and external events all impact the outcomes of your trades.

In both arenas, market forces are unpredictable and dynamic. You cannot control the whims and preferences of Facebook users, just as you cannot always predict or control the profit or loss of your Zerodha trade. In both cases, it is crucial to understand that external factors play a significant role in determining the outcome of your status or trade. While you can exert influence through thoughtful strategies and thorough analysis, there will always be an element of uncertainty.

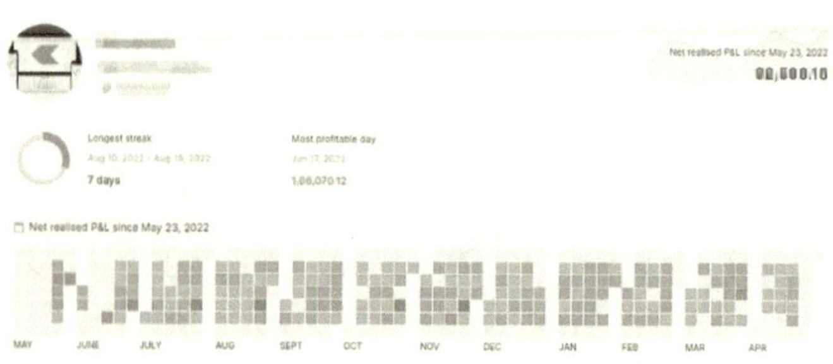

Fig 13: Zerodha Trade - 12 months

It is important to note that just as obsessively checking the number of likes on your Facebook status can be counterproductive and anxiety-inducing, constantly monitoring every movement in the market can lead to impulsive and emotionally driven trading decisions. It is tempting to get caught up in the immediate fluctuations and try to make rapid adjustments to optimize outcomes. However, this can often lead to poor decisions based on short-term noise rather than long-term trends.

Both activities require patience and a balanced perspective. It is essential to keep an eye on the performance of your trade or status, but not to be consumed by every little movement. In social media, some posts gain traction and go viral hours or even days after being shared, emphasizing the importance of patience and giving content time to reach a wider audience. Similarly, in trading, making impulsive decisions based on short-term fluctuations can undermine your overall strategy. It is crucial to have a long-term perspective, to ride out temporary setbacks, and to base your actions on a thorough analysis of market trends.

By recognizing the similarities between posting a status on Facebook and placing a trade in Zerodha, we can approach both activities with a more balanced perspective and increase our chances of success. Understanding that creativity plays a vital role in both endeavors empowers us to think outside the box and find innovative approaches to engage our audience or capitalize on investment opportunities.

Moreover, acknowledging the influence of market forces reminds us that outcomes are not entirely within our control. Just as we cannot dictate the number of likes on our Facebook status, we cannot always dictate the profitability of our trades. Both realms require us to adapt to the ever-changing dynamics of the environment and make informed decisions based on available information.

Developing a patient and disciplined approach is another crucial lesson we can learn from the parallels between social media and financial trading. In the world of social media, expecting instantaneous results and constantly seeking validation can be detrimental to our mental well-being. Similarly, in trading, expecting immediate profits and making impulsive decisions based on short-term market movements can lead to significant losses.

Both activities demand a long-term perspective. In social media, it is important to focus on creating quality content consistently, building a loyal following over time, and engaging with your audience authentically. Likewise, in trading, it is crucial to develop a well-researched investment strategy, diversify your portfolio, and be patient enough to weather temporary setbacks.

> *"I say - Posting a status on Facebook and placing a trade in Zerodha is very much similar*
>
> 1. *Your creativity determines how effective status and trade is*
> 2. *Likes on status and profit on trade is equally determined by market forces*
> 3. *Observing every like and profit closely makes no sense. Be patient and look after a couple of hours*

Furthermore, risk management is a key aspect shared by both social media and financial trading. In the realm of social media, individuals must be mindful of the potential risks associated with sharing personal information, falling prey to misinformation, or encountering online harassment. Similarly, in financial trading, understanding and managing risks, such as market volatility, economic uncertainties, and potential losses, are essential for long-term success.

Education and continuous learning are vital components in both domains. To navigate the ever-evolving landscape of social media, individuals need to stay updated with the latest trends, algorithms, and best practices. Similarly, in trading, staying informed about market news, economic indicators, and industry developments is crucial to making well-informed investment decisions.

Finally, both activities require a degree of self-awareness and emotional intelligence. In the world of social media, being mindful of our intentions, emotions, and the impact of our content on others is key to building meaningful connections and fostering a positive online presence. Similarly, in trading, being aware of our biases, managing emotions such as fear and greed, and maintaining discipline in following our trading plan can significantly improve our decision-making and overall performance.

CHAPTER TWELVE

The Art and Science of Risk Management in Finance

Financial Risk Management is a crucial aspect of the financial world, and it is essential to understand its scientific and artistic aspects. While there are scientific tools and techniques to manage financial risks, it also requires a creative and imaginative approach to conceptualize and implement them effectively. Therefore, financial risk management can be considered both an art and a science.

The scientific aspect of financial risk management involves using quantitative tools and techniques to measure, analyze, and manage risks. These tools include mathematical models, statistical analysis, and computer simulations that help identify and evaluate different types of risks, such as credit risk, market risk, liquidity risk, and operational risk. These tools provide a structured and objective approach to risk management, helping professionals make informed decisions based on data-driven analysis.

For example, in the world of investment banking, professionals use sophisticated models to value financial assets and estimate the risk associated with different investment strategies. These models use historical data, market trends, and other variables to provide a range of potential outcomes and assess the probability of different scenarios. This helps investors and traders make informed decisions and manage their portfolios more effectively.

However, while scientific tools are essential, they are not enough on their own. Financial risk management also requires a creative and imaginative approach to conceptualize and implement these tools effectively. This is where the artistic aspect comes in.

The artistic aspect of financial risk management involves applying creativity, judgment, and intuition to make informed decisions based on scientific analysis. It requires professionals to think critically and imaginatively, considering all the possible outcomes and evaluating the best course of action based on the unique circumstances of each situation.

> *"I say - Financial Risk Management is as much an ART as it is a SCIENCE. For a professional, it is very much required to conceptualize the scientific course and deliver it through the tunnel of artistic talent"*

For example, when managing credit risk, a professional might use a scientific credit rating model to assess the risk of default for a borrower. However, they also need to apply artistic judgment and creativity to understand the context of the borrower's financial situation and evaluate the potential impact of external factors such as changes in interest rates or the economy. This requires a nuanced approach that takes into account both the scientific analysis and the broader market context.

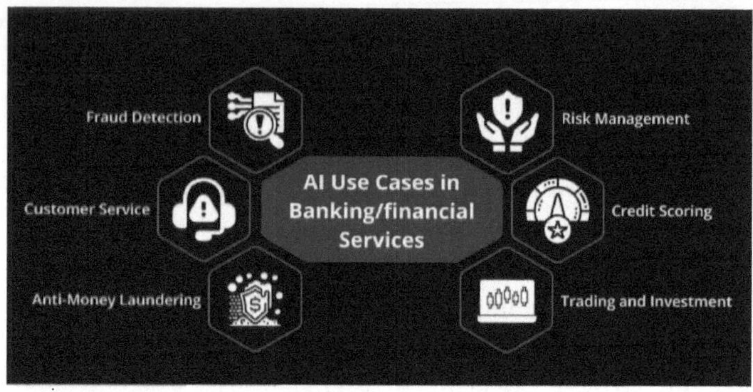

Fig 14: AI use cases in finance

Similarly, in the world of insurance, professionals need to apply artistic judgment to assess the risk of insuring different types of assets. For example, when insuring a building against fire damage, they need to evaluate the building's structural integrity, the materials used in its construction, and the risk of fire based on the building's location and other factors. This requires a creative and imaginative approach that takes into account all the possible scenarios and evaluates the best course of action based on the unique circumstances of each situation.

On top of the AI framework, now Generative AI plays a crucial role in transforming how risks are assessed and managed in the financial sector. Here's a breakdown of its impact:

- In the realm of Fraud Detection and Prevention, Generative AI is utilized to generate synthetic data that mimics real financial transactions. This synthetic data, when combined with authentic data, improves fraud detection algorithms. Simulating different fraudulent scenarios empowers financial institutions to stay ahead of emerging risks and identify potential threats before they materialize.
- Moving on to Risk Assessment, this technology facilitates the creation of realistic financial scenarios by generating synthetic datasets. This supports comprehensive risk assessment, enabling financial analysts to model various market conditions and evaluate potential impacts on portfolios. It enhances the accuracy of risk predictions, contributing to more informed decision-making.
- Generative AI also aids in Market Trends Analysis by generating diverse sets of financial market data. This capability allows institutions to thoroughly analyze historical trends and patterns. Understanding past market behaviors enables financial entities to anticipate future trends, empowering proactive risk management strategies.
- In terms of Personalized Customer Experience, Generative AI creates synthetic customer profiles based on real data. This assists in tailoring financial products and services to individual needs. Beyond enhancing customer satisfaction, this personalized approach mitigates risks associated with offering generic solutions.

- Lastly, in Scenario Modeling, Generative AI facilitates the creation of simulated scenarios for stress testing. Financial institutions can model economic downturns, market crashes, or geopolitical events to evaluate their resilience under adverse conditions. This, in turn, enhances overall risk preparedness within the financial sector.

CHAPTER THIRTEEN

FALSE BILLS AND EXCESSIVE PENALTIES

In the ever-evolving landscape of digital transactions, the synergy between banks and machines plays a pivotal role. However, it's crucial to recognize the inherent distinctions – banks are entities governed by policies, while machines operate within programmed parameters.

1. Banks and Machines: Understanding the Divide Banks and machines serve distinct roles. Expecting machines to comprehend the intricacies of individual financial challenges is unrealistic. It is imperative to acknowledge that machines lack the contextual understanding that humans possess regarding financial nuances

2. Abnormal Escalation in Bills: A Disturbing Trend The manifestation of abnormal spikes in bills and associated penalties, particularly in cases of electricity bills, raises eyebrows. Instances of false bills, seemingly generated by machine errors or potentially fraudulent activities,

can lead to unwarranted financial burdens on consumers.

3. Speaking Up Against False Bills In the face of a false bill, consumers hold the power to initiate change. Raising concerns with the relevant authorities, penning emails, and demanding transparency can pave the way for rectification. It is essential to advocate for accountability and fairness in financial dealings.

4. The Machine's Brain: Unveiling the Inquiry Machines, though devoid of consciousness, possess a programmed intelligence. Conducting a thorough inquiry into false billing instances can serve as a teaching moment for machines. Understanding the root cause and rectifying the programming errors contributes to a more accurate and ethical financial system.

5. Auto-Debit Caution: A Shield Against Fraud For those relying on auto-debit features, vigilance is key. In anticipation of fraudulent bills, proactive steps such as requesting the removal of auto-debit instructions or utilizing a different bank account can act as a safeguard. This empowers individuals to maintain control over their financial transactions.

6. Human Action in Accounting Mechanics Human actions shape the mechanics of the accounting infrastructure. The flow of information, decisions, and ethical conduct influence the functioning of both banks and machines. Individuals are encouraged to take decisive action against any unethical or unlawful practices, contributing to a more transparent and just financial ecosystem.

Fig 15: Fake invoice - raise complaints

The collaboration between banks and machines is a dynamic interplay that demands vigilance and active participation from consumers. While machines are powerful tools, human oversight, and ethical engagement are pivotal to ensuring a fair and reliable financial system. It is through collective awareness and action that we can navigate the complexities of modern banking, mitigating the impact of false bills and excessive penalties.

> *"I say - Garbage In Garbage Out (GIGO) principle applies to the machine control financial system too. Pitch in the right customs and machine will print righteous bills and with bad intensions, it can print bogus ones."*

Machine learning (ML) has become an integral component of various financial processes, as discussed earlier. Drawing insights from the previous discourse on machines and the financial system, let's delve into the specific applications and roles of machine learning in finance:

1. Managing Assets and Risk Evaluation: Machine learning algorithms play a crucial role in managing assets by analyzing historical data and market trends to optimize investment portfolios. This aligns with the broader understanding that machines lack the nuanced understanding of individual financial challenges, necessitating intelligent systems to make informed decisions.

2. Fraud Detection: One of the widely adopted applications of machine learning in finance is fraud detection. ML algorithms analyze patterns and anomalies in transactions, helping to identify potentially fraudulent activities. This aligns with the caution advised against fraudulent bills, emphasizing the importance of vigilance and proactive measures.

3. Risk Assessment and Regulatory Compliance: Machine learning aids in risk assessment by analyzing vast datasets to predict potential risks. Moreover, it contributes to regulatory compliance by automating processes and ensuring adherence to financial regulations. This echoes the discussion on human action

shaping the mechanics of the accounting infrastructure, emphasizing ethical conduct and compliance.

4. Customer Service and Process Automation: ML applications enhance customer service by providing personalized insights and recommendations. Additionally, process automation is streamlined through machine learning, ensuring efficient and error-free financial operations. This relates to the idea that machines, although lacking consciousness, possess programmed intelligence that can be refined through proper inquiry.

Fig 16: Process Improvement in Machine Implementation

In essence, machine learning acts as a catalyst in the financial realm, addressing the limitations of machines and enhancing the efficiency, accuracy, and transparency of financial processes. Its applications align with the challenges discussed earlier, emphasizing the need for proactive measures, human oversight, and ethical engagement in the ever-evolving landscape of finance.

CHAPTER FOURTEEN

TRADITIONAL AI VS. GENERATIVE AI

The quote "Traditional AI is like a rocket that will take you to the stars. Whereas Generative AI is like a black hole that can route you to an unknown galaxy" draws an analogy to highlight the distinctive characteristics of Traditional AI and Generative AI.

Fig 17: The rocket launched toward a star into Milky Way

Traditional AI as a Rocket:

Explanation: Traditional AI is likened to a rocket because, like a rocket with a predefined trajectory, it follows set rules and algorithms to achieve specific tasks. It excels in structured data analysis and task automation.

Example: In finance, Traditional AI may be applied to predict market trends or automate routine tasks with well-defined rules.

Generative AI as a Black Hole:

Explanation: Generative AI is compared to a black hole because it can create novel and unforeseen outcomes. Similar to how a black hole's gravitational pull can lead to unexplored regions, Generative AI goes beyond predefined rules, fostering innovation in content creation and data generation.

Example: OpenAI's GPT-3 is a Generative AI model capable of generating diverse and contextually relevant text based on prompts, demonstrating creativity in content generation.

> *"I say - Traditional AI is like a rocket that will take you to the stars. Whereas Generative AI is like a black hole that can route you to an unknown galaxy."*

So, let's dive into the implications of traditional AI and Gen AI.

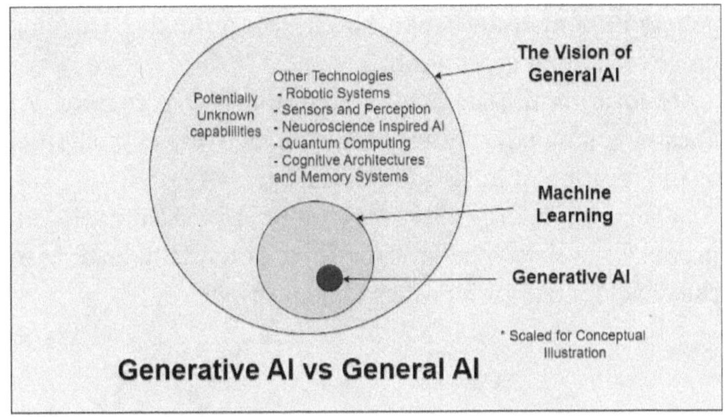

Fig 18: Gen AI Vs. Tradiational AI

Traditional AI:

Data Analysis: Traditional AI is proficient in analyzing existing datasets to extract valuable insights and predict future trends.

Example: In finance, traditional AI algorithms analyze historical market data to predict stock prices and guide investment decisions.

Task Automation: Traditional AI is extensively used for automating routine tasks based on predefined rules and algorithms.

Example: Robotic Process Automation (RPA) systems use traditional AI to automate repetitive tasks like data entry, reducing human workload.

Generative AI:

Content Creation: Generative AI specializes in creating new and original content, ranging from text and images to music and art.

Example: OpenAI's GPT-3, a generative AI model, can generate human-like text based on prompts, enabling creative content generation.

Innovation in Data: Unlike traditional AI, generative AI goes beyond analyzing existing data, actively contributing to the creation of innovative datasets.

Example: In drug discovery, generative AI models can propose novel molecular structures, potentially leading to the development of innovative medications.

About Prabhat Kumar

Born in 1985 in Dhanbad, Bihar, the author completed his initial schooling from Dhanbad only. Throughout his time in school, the author demonstrated excellence, presenting over 10 papers at national-level competitions when he was at VIT University. Even though he could have gone to a prestigious college (at IIT (ISM) Dhanbad) in 2003, he chose to stay at VIT in Vellore to follow his love for research and fun activities.

Later, he worked in big tech companies and international banks, learning a lot about how technology and money work together. In 2023, his work in education got noticed, and ML360 Educations became the best Edu Tech Company according to MSME of Karnataka.

The author does research in different areas, especially focusing on how cryptocurrency works. He also helps others by coaching and training in Testing, Finance, and Data Science. He finished a special program in Applied Machine Learning from Columbia Engineering.

Besides work, the author loves arts and music. He expresses his creativity through a blog and YouTube channel called "Meri Madhushala." He started ML360 Educations to teach finance and machine learning and also made a consulting website called Analyst Prabhat.

He wrote two books, "Meri Madhushala" and "Nectars of Life." The books have emotional poetry and promise to explore machine learning, finance, testing, and data science in a very careful way, giving practical uses and real-life examples. The author wants everyone, especially students and enthusiasts, to read his books and learn together.

...

Important Links
Facebook: https://www.facebook.com/pkc.prabhat
LinkedIn: https://www.linkedin.com/in/pkprabhat
X (Twitter): https://twitter.com/pkcprabhat
Instagram: https://www.instagram.com/poetprabhat
Website: https://www.analystprabhat.in
Appointments: https://www.analystprabhat.com
Contact Us: contactprabhatkumar@gmail.com